VOL. NO. 1

CHANGE YOUR WORLD

**INSPIRATION TO EMPOWER
THE CHURCH IN THE
MARKETPLACE**

Copyright © 2021 by Inspire

Published by Inspire

All rights reserved. No portion of this book may be reproduced, stored in a retrieval system, or transmitted in any form or by any means—electronic, mechanical, photocopy, recording, scanning, or other—except for brief quotations in critical reviews or articles, without prior written permission of the author.

For foreign and subsidiary rights, contact the author.

Cover and interior design by Joe De Leon
Compiled by Andy Green

ISBN: 978-1-954089-82-2   1 2 3 4 5 6 7 8 9 10

Printed in the United States of America

VOL. NO.1 —

CHANGE YOUR WORLD

**INSPIRATION TO EMPOWER
THE CHURCH IN THE
MARKETPLACE**

INSPIRE

CONTENTS

Introduction 7

1. Growth 9

2. Insight 33

3. Reflection 55

4. Wisdom 75

5. Purpose 93

6. Commitment 119

7. Inspiration 137

8. Gifts 153

INTRODUCTION

It's been said that the Christian life is summed up in Micah 6:8: "He has shown you, O mortal, what is good. And what does the Lord require of you? To act justly and to love mercy and to walk humbly with your God." It's a theme echoed in Amos 5:15: "Hate evil, love good; maintain justice in the courts."

For both these Old Testament prophets, our relationship with God should spill out into the world around us. It's not enough to simply hold to biblical truths; we need to actively express them in some way. Acting justly and maintaining justice involve doing things in our everyday lives.

With the number of "Nones"—people who don't identify with a particular religious tradition—continuing to grow, many people will never come to a church service to hear the good news of the gospel. But they may get to see the church in action through believers who live out their faith at their workplace and in their communities.

This is marketplace ministry—Christians following God's leading into all areas of life, from business and education to the arts and education, politics and medicine. It's the church Monday through Saturday, and it's drawing more and more people who want to be part of a new expression of God's kingdom.

The Inspire Collective was founded to encourage and equip believers to live out their calling to be influencers and change-makers wherever that may take them. Through the pages of *Inspire* magazine, we have told stories of how men and women have pursued their vision to make a difference.

In *Change Your World: Inspiration to Empower the Church in the Marketplace*, we have gathered some of their insights, experiences, and lessons to fuel your journey as you respond to Micah's and Amos's admonition. May these highlights point the way for you as you seek to influence culture and impact change in your world.

—Andy Butcher
Editorial Director, Inspire Collective

GROWTH

CHANGE YOUR WORLD

9

SO TO ME, IF YOU WANT TO GROW YOUR CHURCH, YOU HAVE TO GROW YOURSELF. AND FOR ME, THIS HAS BEEN FOURTEEN YEARS OF MY PERSONAL GROWTH.

Kenneth Claytor

••••

INSPIRE PODCAST

WHAT MISTAKES HAVE YOU MADE IN THE PAST? LEARN FROM THOSE MISTAKES, AND DON'T REPEAT THEM. **WHAT DIDN'T WORK FOR YOU?** FIND A NEW WAY OF DOING IT. **WE TYPICALLY LEARN NOT THROUGH BEING SUCCESSFUL RIGHT AWAY, BUT BY TRYING OVER AND OVER AGAIN UNTIL WE GET IT RIGHT.**

Dr. Chris Bowen

••••

THE 5-STAR ENTREPRENEUR

Leaders will only grow to the threshold of their pain.

Dr. Sam Chand

LADDER LEADERS

You don't need a magic wand to change your narrative. Take steps in the right direction, and trust God to be the author and finisher of your faith.

Lisa Kai

....

INSPIRE MAGAZINE, SPRING 2021 ISSUE

> Sometimes we take the path of least resistance, but that stunts our growth. The lessons and character built through the process (are) what will set you up for future success and make you a better person. We need to embrace the process because that's where we will be refined and be successful.
>
> Bryan Clay

INSPIRE MAGAZINE, *SPRING 2021 ISSUE*

GROWTH

I WAS SO BUSY TRYING TO LEAD EVERY PART OF MY BUSINESS THAT I TOOK ON THE BURDEN OF THE ENTIRE ORGANIZATION'S RESULTS. I QUICKLY LEARNED THAT FOR ME TO BETTER LEAD OUR ORGANIZATION, I NEEDED TO LEARN HOW TO LEAD MYSELF FIRST.

Micah Cravalho

••••

INSPIRE MAGAZINE, SPRING 2021 ISSUE

> I feel like the faster I can grow personally and get over myself, learn and really excel, and just take the next steps, then the company kind of comes with it.

Derek Dienner

. . . .

INSPIRE MAGAZINE, SPRING 2021 ISSUE

GROWTH

> So many people say that the reason I'm here on the executive team is because I'm a woman, but as a woman I deserve a seat at the table. The world doesn't just give you things. I had to learn and develop as a CEO.

Marissa Bell

••••

INSPIRE MAGAZINE, *SPRING 2021 ISSUE*

THE STARK REALITY IS THAT LEADERSHIP DEVELOPMENT IS NOT AN EVENT. IT'S AN ONGOING PROCESS OF PREPARING FOR HARVESTING. THE BEST RESULTS ALWAYS COME TO THOSE WHO ARE MOST PREPARED.

Nicholas John

PILOT

GROWTH

Be flexible and be available. By flexible, I mean teachable. There is still so much I need to learn. I need help. I'm better off when I admit I don't know everything about business.

Gus Mello

* * * *

INSPIRE MAGAZINE, *SUMMER 2021 ISSUE*

ON YOUR JOURNEY TO BECOMING THE PERSON YOU WERE MEANT TO BE, THERE ARE CERTAIN TESTS THAT WILL UNDENIABLY SHOW UP IN YOUR LIFE IN SOME FORM OR FASHION. YOU MUST PASS THEM TO QUALIFY FOR PROMOTION TO YOUR NEXT LEVEL.

Robert Watkins

. . . .

CHOSEN

GROWTH

Every pain and every setback is a classroom for us to learn life's biggest lessons.

Dr. Brenda Chand

••••

YOU *CAN* COACH

> So much of what we know lies dormant inside of us, waiting to be pulled out.

Martijn van Tilborgh

• • • •

UNLEASHED

GROWTH

You must constantly reinvent yourself.

Mike Kai

....

IT DOESN'T JUST HAPPEN

I ALWAYS WANT TO DO SOMETHING THAT'S UNCOMFORTABLE. SOMETHING THAT'S GOING TO STRETCH ME, SO I NEED TO RELY ON HIM.

Gus Mello

• • • •
INSPIRE PODCAST

GROWTH

HERE'S WHAT I'VE LEARNED. PEOPLE WHO FAIL FORWARD, LOVE TO SHARE THEIR FAILURES. . . . I'M SO GLAD YOU'RE A TEACHER. I'M SO GLAD YOU ARE A PROFESSOR. I'M SO GLAD THAT YOU CAN BRING THAT WISDOM.

Josh Duhaylonsod

You take those lemons, and you decide what you're going to do.

Kim Schofield

····

INSPIRE PODCAST

> I believe if you want to be a lifelong learner, always learn because knowledge truly is pleasing to God if you do it right.

Mike Mathews

INSPIRE PODCAST

What you pour in is what you get out. I absolutely love to learn. I love to learn new things, so I do see the beauty of learning. My husband has this quote: "Everything healthy grows, and everything that grows changes." Knowing that this thing called life is ever-changing, ever-evolving, I always want to grow.

Ty Moody

• • • •

INSPIRE MAGAZINE, *SUMMER 2021 ISSUE*

GROWTH

Be patient. . . . . I wanted to be everything at once. Just enjoy the season you're in because in this season (you're) being formed and prepared for what's to come.

Christian Taylor

. . . .

INSPIRE MAGAZINE, *SUMMER 2021 ISSUE*

GOD IS NOT OBLIGATED TO "BLESS" SOMETHING YOU CREATE. HE DOES, HOWEVER, MAKE HIMSELF RESPONSIBLE FOR COMPLETING WHAT HE STARTS. SO ASK, "LORD, WHAT ARE YOU UP TO? WHERE DO I FIT IN THE STORY YOU ARE WRITING? WHAT NEXT STEP DO YOU NEED ME TO TAKE?"

Carol Tanksley

• • • •

***INSPIRE MAGAZINE**, SPRING 2021 ISSUE*

GROWTH

YOU MIGHT LEARN THAT YOU'VE BEEN TRYING TO PRAY YOUR WAY OUT OF THE VERY PLACE GOD HAS PURPOSED YOU FOR. **HE CREATED YOU WITH PURPOSE AND DESTINY.** IT'S ABOUT LETTING GO AND ALLOWING YOUR CREATOR TO SHOW YOU WHO HE CREATED YOU TO BE.

Ada Madison

• • • •

INSPIRE MAGAZINE, SUMMER 2021 ISSUE

INSIGHT

CHANGE YOUR WORLD

CHANGE YOUR WORLD

PLAY

WHAT IF YOU COULD HAVE IT BOTH WAYS—IF YOU COULD PLAY WHILE AT WORK AND WORK DURING YOUR TIME OFF?

Josh Duhaylonsod

••••
INSPIRE MAGAZINE, *SPRING 2021 ISSUE*

INSIGHT

PARTNER WITH GOD IN YOUR MARRIAGE, YOUR BUSINESS, YOUR HEALTH, AND YOUR JOB. GOD'S UP TO SOMETHING. THAT FOCUS CHANGES EVERYTHING.

Carol Tanksley

• • • •

INSPIRE MAGAZINE, SPRING 2021 ISSUE

Music is the soundtrack to our lives, and I think we undervalue the power it has. Music can reach our deepest mental and spiritual areas.

Montell Jordan

CHANGE YOUR WORLD

INSPIRE MAGAZINE, SPRING 2021 ISSUE

INSIGHT

> Science and faith don't conflict. . . . They're always in lockstep. It's when one does not appreciate the truth of the other one, that's the problem, but they are not oppositional.
>
> Bishop Horace E. Smith, M.D.

....

INSPIRE MAGAZINE, SPRING 2021 ISSUE

> **WE NEED TO STOP OVERCOMPLICATING THIS. WHAT YOU NEED TO DO IS GO INTO YOUR PRAYER CLOSET, CLOSE THE DOOR, AND PRAY TO GOD.**
>
> John Houston

• • • •

INSPIRE MAGAZINE, SPRING 2021 ISSUE

INSIGHT

PROVERBS NOT ONLY INDICATES THE CHARACTERISTICS, SKILLS, AND PRACTICES OF A GODLY BUSINESS VENTURE, BUT ALSO THE EXPECTED OUTCOMES. ECHOING ECCLESIASTES, PROVERBS REVEALS THAT WEALTH, POSSESSION, AND THE ABILITY TO ENJOY THEM AND BE HAPPY IN WORK ARE GIFTS FROM GOD.

Hannah J. Stolze

• • • •

WISDOM-BASED BUSINESS: APPLYING BIBLICAL PRINCIPLES AND EVIDENCE-BASED RESEARCH FOR A PURPOSEFUL AND PROFITABLE BUSINESS (ZONDERVAN)

You see, there is a vast difference between preparing and planning. You plan for a wedding day, but you prepare for a lifetime of marriage. You plan for a baby, but you prepare for a family.

Nicholas John

PILOT

INSIGHT

People have bought into the lie that they have to do world-changing things to change the world. That they have to be seen and known and "successful" in order to make a real difference. But that's simply not true. As I have learned unexpectedly, you just need to show up and "Let your light so shine before men, that they may see your good works and glorify your Father in heaven" (Matthew 5:16).

Billy Ivey

• • • •

INSPIRE MAGAZINE, SUMMER 2021 ISSUE

> YOU HAVE TO REALIZE YOU HAVE A ROLE TO PLAY, BUT THERE'S SOMETHING ELSE HAPPENING. THERE ARE WANTS, NEEDS, DESIRES, AND SUCCESS TRACKS THAT CLEARLY YOU WANT TO HAPPEN. . . . THERE IS ANOTHER PART THAT IS OUT OF YOUR CONTROL, OR AS I WOULD SAY THAT IS IN YOUR FAITH BUCKET, THAT YOU HAVE TO BE ABLE TO DIP INTO.

Louis Carr

• • • •

INSPIRE MAGAZINE, SUMMER 2021 ISSUE

INSIGHT

What you feed grows, and what you starve dies.

Dr. Dave Martin

• • • •

MAKE THAT, BREAK THAT

YOU SEE, THERE IS A VAST DIFFERENCE BETWEEN PREPARING AND PLANNING. YOU PLAN FOR A WEDDING DAY, BUT YOU PREPARE FOR A LIFETIME OF MARRIAGE. YOU PLAN FOR A BABY, BUT YOU PREPARE FOR A FAMILY.

Nicholas John

....

PILOT

WHAT HINDERS US OTHER THAN SIN? OUR HEARTS. WITHIN US MIGHT BE SELF-DOUBT, A NEED FOR CONTROL, FEAR OF FAILURE, JADEDNESS WITH OTHERS, A MISTRUST IN GOD'S LOVE OR RELIANCE ON THINGS TURNING OUT WELL TO BE WELL. **THERE IS SO MUCH IN OUR HEARTS THAT DOESN'T SEPARATE US FROM GOD AS SIN DOES, BUT THAT DOESN'T REFLECT GOD EITHER.**

Dr. Charity Byers

> There were things that people saw in me that I didn't see myself. . . . (God put) the right people in my life and His hand of favor on my life.
>
> Ty Moody

INSIGHT

> Neither of us would be natural decision-makers, but, nine times out of ten, whether you decide A or B as your route is less significant than making a decision and getting on with it. All else being equal, there is often not a right and a wrong choice. Making a choice and moving forward has been key for us. This is probably where we've found our mojo clearest.
>
> Jonathan and Sarah Bamber

> IT'S THE BUSINESS OF THE KINGDOM. ... JESUS IS THE EMPHASIS. AND WE HAVE TO BUILD A TEAM AND USE ALL OF THE SAME PRINCIPLES TO GET THAT MESSAGE OUT AS (WE) WOULD IN NATURAL BUSINESS. THE BIG DIFFERENCE IS THAT IN THE BUSINESS WORLD, I DIDN'T NECESSARILY HAVE THE DEVIL TRYING TO KILL ME.

Kenneth Claytor

· · · ·

INSPIRE PODCAST

INSIGHT

MY RESPONSIBILITY IS TO TAKE ADVANTAGE OF THE OPPORTUNITY TO ENGAGE. WHAT HAPPENS WITH THAT— WHAT GOD CHOOSES TO DO WITH THAT OR WHO CHOOSES TO CONNECT WITH THAT—IS NOT MY RESPONSIBILITY.

Billy Ivey

• • • •

INSPIRE PODCAST

Yes, I know, the Bible says man looks at the outward appearance; God looks at the heart. However, people may never get a chance to know your heart as well if you don't make a lasting impression on them in what you say, how you look, and what you do.

Mike Kai

....

IT DOESN'T JUST HAPPEN

INSIGHT

Here's the challenge. You can only give what you have. You can't pass on what you don't possess because you tend to teach the way you were taught. Are you going to inflict the same accidental leadership on the next generation? Or are you going to have a plan?

Dr. Sam Chand

• • • •

LADDER LEADERS

THE OLD PHRASE, "KEEP IT SIMPLE" IS STILL GOOD ADVICE. IF OUR TO-DO LIST IS TOO LARGE, WE GET FRUSTRATED AND GIVE UP. WE NEED TO LOOK AT OUR LIST AND PRIORITIZE WHAT'S MOST IMPORTANT, SO WE CAN AVOID BECOMING OVERWHELMED.

Dr. Brenda Chand

....

YOU CAN COACH

INSIGHT

Dreams applied—but distorted to serve the self—lead only to chaos and evil in all areas of life.

Allison van Tilborgh

Complexity and misguided structure can make a simple task laborious and difficult.

Krystal Parker

CHANGE YOUR WORLD

THE BEST ROBOT WINS

REFLECTION

CHANGE YOUR WORLD

> It's vital for an organization to use measurements and controls to help their employees be successful in their jobs but not at the expense of removing their ability to feel that they matter as humans.

Krystal Parker

REFLECTION

Until you know where you stand, you cannot know where you're going. Until you know what you lack, you cannot know what you need. That is why it would be wise to enlist the help of others as you take a hard look at the destructive habits that rule your life, and that is why you need to spend some "alone time" as you think about the behaviors you would like to adopt instead.

Dr. Dave Martin

....

MAKE THAT, BREAK THAT

WHEN CHRIST IS REVEALED TO US ON A PERSONAL LEVEL, THAT REVELATION BECOMES REALER THAN ANY CIRCUMSTANCE AND REALITY AROUND US. WHEN THIS HAPPENS, YOU CAN TRULY START YOUR WALK WITH GOD.

Martijn van Tilborgh

• • • •

UNLEASHED

Remember, we may plan all the answers, but it's the questions we don't know.

Nicholas John

· · · ·

NICHOLAS JOHN

The most important conversations are always going to be the ones we have with ourselves.

Dr. Sam Chand

• • • •

LADDER LEADERS

REFLECTION

WHAT SEPARATES AN EXCELLENT LEADER FROM AN AVERAGE LEADER IS THAT THE LATTER FIGURES OUT WHY THEIR SYSTEMS AND STRUCTURES ARE NOT WORKING AND IMPROVES THEM.

Mike Kai

• • • •

IT DOESN'T JUST HAPPEN

I cannot claim that I changed that kid's life in that moment, but I changed that moment in that kid's life. That was a powerful reminder that we all have a special opportunity to engage in ways that we might not ever see evidence of

Billy Ivey

....

INSPIRE PODCAST

REFLECTION

God's always put me in impossible situations to be that voice for the voiceless. I sometimes have to stand alone. I have to make sure that I have the courage to say, "I'm going to do the right thing regardless," because at the end of the day, I'd rather be in with God and out with man than in with man and out with God.

Kim Schofield

* * * *

INSPIRE PODCAST

That's the hard part about not being able to rewrite your story. Some people want to keep writing and writing and writing but never finishing a chapter. I always feel like, You just missed the best part of the chapter— the hardship or the struggles. It's okay just to walk it through— walk through the pain, walk through the insecurity, or even walk through things that you just don't know what to do (with) . . . to see what it could be.

Lisa Kai

• • • •

INSPIRE PODCAST

REFLECTION

JUST TALKING TO PEOPLE WHO HAVE BEEN THERE AND CAN GIVE YOU THAT VERY PRACTICAL ADVICE TO DEAL WITH CERTAIN THINGS OR HOW TO DEAL WITH CERTAIN ISSUES . . . REALLY HELPS A LOT.

Tricia Goyer

• • • •

INSPIRE PODCAST

STARTING SMALL IS OKAY. WE HAVE THIS VISION, AND IT'S GRAND, AND WE WANT TO JUST GET THERE. I HAD TO LEARN THAT SMALL VICTORIES ARE GREAT, AND YOU DON'T HAVE TO HAVE EVERYTHING RIGHT NOW.

Ty Moody

• • • •

INSPIRE PODCAST

REFLECTION

> The single greatest contribution to the success I have enjoyed in building a successful family of companies over the past near-twenty years has been a daily practice of actively seeking God's direction and then doing what He says.
>
> John Houston

INSPIRE MAGAZINE, SUMMER 2021 ISSUE

The best thing you can do when you have experienced a failure in your life is to understand what went wrong, learn from your mistakes, and try again with the newfound knowledge that you did not possess the first time around. As you honestly evaluate your past misses, ask yourself what role teamwork may have played in your temporary failure.

Dr. Dave Martin

....

INSPIRE MAGAZINE, SUMMER 2021 ISSUE

REFLECTION

MY FAITH HAS GIVEN ME SOMETHING TO LEAN ON. EACH DAY HAS A ROLLER COASTER OF EMOTIONS AND NEW CHALLENGES, BUT I AM TRUSTING GOD THROUGH IT ALL AND HUMBLY WAITING TO SEE WHAT HE HAS IN STORE FOR ME NEXT.

Christian Taylor

• • • •

INSPIRE MAGAZINE, SUMMER 2021 ISSUE

I pray that God would give me insight into a character, into a scenario that would give me some creative options, and that I would come up with ideas that I never could have on my own. The blend of what the Lord does and what I do—if there is any separation at all—is too intertwined for me to decipher.

Steven Lane

I take a trip down memory lane and think about all those people who injected themselves into my life, who did something they did not need to do. It still gives me a chill to think about some of the things that they did, and that motivates me to do it for somebody else.

Louis Carr

THE BIBLE ENCOURAGES US TO FIND OUR PURPOSE. THE PASTORS I WORK WITH REMIND ME OF THESE THINGS. NO OTHER STARTUP CEO GETS PRAYED FOR AS MUCH AS I DO, AND IT MAKES ME STRONGER.

Marissa Bell

• • • •

INSPIRE MAGAZINE, SPRING 2021 ISSUE

REFLECTION

Remember, the goal is to stand out. Think about what you have done.

Crystal Marshall

. . . .

INSPIRE MAGAZINE, *SPRING 2021 ISSUE*

EVEN THOUGH I HAVE WORKED ON SUPERCOMPUTERS AND EXPERIENCED SOME OF THE MOST AMAZING TECHNOLOGICAL ADVANCES, I STILL RECOGNIZE THAT OUR SENSORY FACULTIES—HEART, BRAIN, AND SPIRIT—MAKE UP THE CULMINATION OF INTELLIGENCE PERCEIVED BY OUR MIND'S EYE.

Mike Mathews

• • • •

INSPIRE MAGAZINE, SPRING 2021 ISSUE

WISDOM

Unquestionably, some mainstream news media coverage of political and social issues has become increasingly partisan. What were even recently traditionally held conservative views and values are now routinely portrayed as extreme. But for Christians to dismiss out of hand as "fake news" everything they'd prefer not to hear is far too simplistic.

Andy Butcher

• • • •

INSPIRE MAGAZINE, SPRING 2021 ISSUE

WISDOM

Look for the moments in your workday that can enrich the rest of your life. Be open to ideas and creative solutions for work that you may come across in your "off" time. "Clock in" or "clock out" for a few moments as appropriate, and then return to what you are doing, whether that's at work or at home.

Josh Duhaylonsod

....

INSPIRE MAGAZINE, SPRING 2021 ISSUE

Focus on the actions you can take. Leave the outcomes to God.

Carol Tanksley

····

INSPIRE MAGAZINE, *SPRING 2021 ISSUE*

WISDOM

YOU HAVE TO UNDERSTAND AND KNOW YOUR GOAL. YOU HAVE TO LEARN HOW TO FOCUS. THEN YOU HAVE TO BUILD A PLAN AND SURROUND YOURSELF WITH GOOD PEOPLE. THERE'S NO MAGIC TO IT. YOU SET YOURSELF UP TO BE SUCCESSFUL.

Bryan Clay

• • • •

INSPIRE MAGAZINE, SPRING 2021 ISSUE

Be flexible and be available. By flexible, I mean teachable. There is still so much I need to learn. I need help. I'm better off when I admit I don't know everything about business.

Gus Mello

INSPIRE MAGAZINE, SUMMER 2021 ISSUE

WISDOM

> I'm good at a certain amount of things, and then (I need to) find people to do all the things that aren't my strengths. Then (I have to) be willing to hand those things over and lay my ego down and just have the team find the solutions for me and help me get there

Derek Dienner

• • • •

INSPIRE MAGAZINE, SPRING 2021 ISSUE

THE HEAVENS DECLARE THE GLORY OF GOD. . . . THE HEAVENS ARE SYSTEMATIC, THEY'RE IN ORDER. THE PLANETS AND STARS ARE PHENOMENAL, THEY FOLLOW PHYSICAL SCIENCE. AND I WOULD SAY THAT COULDN'T HAPPEN BY CHANCE. THAT HAD TO BE BY A CREATOR WITH A DELIBERATE PLAN. SO I BELIEVE IN SCIENCE.

Bishop Horace E. Smith, M.D.

• • • •

INSPIRE MAGAZINE, SPRING 2021 ISSUE

With all that is on my plate, it would be easy to get up and immediately jump into work mode, but I know I need to start the day by listening to God.

John Houston

....

INSPIRE MAGAZINE, *SUMMER 2021 ISSUE*

OPTIMIZING THE VISIONARY ISN'T ABOUT BUILDING MORE LEADERSHIP SKILLS. IT'S NOT ABOUT THE TOP TEN STRATEGIES FOR TEAM-BUILDING, INNOVATION, AND VISION-CASTING. IT'S ABOUT FREEING YOUR HEART FROM ALL THAT HOLDS IT BACK AND WEIGHS IT DOWN.

Dr. Charity Byers

• • • •

INSPIRE MAGAZINE, SUMMER 2021 ISSUE

WISDOM

REMEMBER, DON'T PRAY FOR PATIENCE. PATIENCE, ACCORDING TO THE BOOK OF JAMES, COMES THROUGH MANY TRIALS AND TRIBULATIONS. SO TRY TO BE PATIENT WITHOUT PRAYING FOR IT.

Dr. Chris Bowen

· · · ·

THE 5-STAR ENTREPRENEUR

> The point is that unless we open up and benefit from the wisdom of others, we're apt to make unwise decisions.
>
> Dr. Sam Chand
>
> ....
>
> **LADDER LEADERS**

WISDOM

> If wisdom builds a house, then a lack of wisdom can tear it down. If excellence and great customer service can build a brand, then forsaking those values can bring it to an abrupt halt.
>
> Mike Kai

....
IT DOESN'T JUST HAPPEN

> If you try to please the unpleasable, you're embarking on an endless journey—an unwinnable battle.
>
> Martijn van Tilborgh

UNLEASHED

WISDOM

I NEED LEADERS TO UNDERSTAND A WAY TO STRIKE A BALANCE BETWEEN STRATEGY AND LEADERSHIP; IT IS NONNEGOTIABLE. IF THAT SEEMS COLD OR IMPERSONAL TO YOU, I WOULD SAY, "IT AIN'T PERSONAL, IT'S JUST BUSINESS."

Krystal Parker

• • • •

THE BEST ROBOT WINS

We are committed to the long haul, and I have learned an important lesson along the way for anyone pursuing a vision, whether it's in ministry, business or some other area of their life. It's this: The results are not your responsibility.

Micah Cravalho

....

INSPIRE MAGAZINE, SPRING 2021 ISSUE

WISDOM

God may put a specific calling or vision on your heart without giving you all of the details. Like Joshua leading the children of Israel into the Promised Land, we often have to step out in faith and trust that God will fill in the blanks as we go.

Christine Caine

• • • •

INSPIRE MAGAZINE, SPRING 2021 ISSUE

Proverbs not only indicates the characteristics, skills and practices of a godly business venture, but also the expected outcomes. Echoing Ecclesiastes, Proverbs reveals that wealth, possession, and the ability to enjoy them and be happy in work are gifts from God.

Hannah J. Stolze

....

WISDOM-BASED BUSINESS: APPLYING BIBLICAL PRINCIPLES AND EVIDENCE-BASED RESEARCH FOR A PURPOSEFUL AND PROFITABLE BUSINESS (ZONDERVAN)

PURPOSE

CHANGE YOUR WORLD

THE MAINSTREAM MEDIA ISN'T GOING TO GO AWAY JUST BECAUSE BELIEVERS IGNORE IT. IT'S GOING TO KEEP DOING ITS JOB, WHICH IN ONE WAY IS THE SAME AS THE CHURCH'S: DISCIPLESHIP. MAKING FOLLOWERS.

Andy Butcher

• • • •

INSPIRE MAGAZINE, SPRING 2021 ISSUE

GOD HAS CREATED EACH ONE OF US ON PURPOSE, FOR A PURPOSE, AND PURSUING OUR PURPOSE REQUIRES COURAGE AND FAITH.

Christine Caine

• • • •

INSPIRE MAGAZINE, *SPRING 2021 ISSUE*

God calls us to be excellent in what we do.

Bryan Clay

••••

INSPIRE MAGAZINE, SPRING 2021 ISSUE

CHANGE YOUR WORLD

EXCELLENT

PURPOSE

God has called you to make a difference in the world for his kingdom. Let that knowledge be fuel in your soul to keep you walking forward. Your feelings of failure aren't the end of the story. God is writing the next chapter, and you've got a role to play.

Carol Tanksley

INSPIRE MAGAZINE, SPRING 2021 ISSUE

> A LOT OF PEOPLE ARE USING THEIR TALENTS, BUT THEY'RE USING THEM IN AREAS THAT THEY'RE NOT NECESSARILY ANOINTED TO USE THEM IN. I WAS GIFTED BY GOD TO BE ABLE TO ENTERTAIN, BUT THAT WASN'T MY PURPOSE OR MY CALLING. MY CALLING IS TO DO MINISTRY.
>
> Montell Jordan

INSPIRE MAGAZINE, SPRING 2021 ISSUE

PURPOSE

LOSING FAITH IS ONE OF THE MOST UNFORTUNATE EVENTS THAT COULD HAPPEN TO YOU. WITHOUT FAITH, YOU LOSE HOPE, AND THEN BECOME HOPELESS. WHEN ADVERSITY PRESENTS ITSELF, IT'S REALLY A TEST OF FAITH, TO FIND OUT IF YOU REALLY BELIEVE IN WHAT YOU'RE DOING.

Robert Watkins

• • • •

CHOSEN

We can kind of measure (success) by our accolades, what we do, but through faith, it's actually who you are—who God has allowed you to be and the platform He has given you. . . . As long as I'm using my platform to share His love, to share who He is and the peace that comes with that, that is really my focus.

Christian Taylor

• • • •

INSPIRE MAGAZINE, SUMMER 2021 ISSUE

PURPOSE

There were times I cried out to God, "Is this really what you are asking of me? I'm not sure I can stay the course!" Yet time and time again God provided the peace, the strength, and the faith to take the next step and pour love out onto my kids one more day. God doesn't ask us to save the world, but He does ask us to pour out our lives for others.

Tricia Goyer

WE ARE IN A PIVOTAL MOMENT TO EMBRACE TECHNOLOGY TO HELP FULFILL THE NEEDS OF PEOPLE AND HOPEFULLY GROW THE CHURCH.

Marissa Bell

• • • •

INSPIRE MAGAZINE, SPRING 2021 ISSUE

PURPOSE

God doesn't ask us to save the world, but He does ask us to pour out our lives for others.

Tricia Goyer

. . . .

INSPIRE MAGAZINE, SUMMER 2021 ISSUE

OUR MISSION AS A COUPLE IS TO HONOR GOD BY DEDICATING OUR LIVES TO THE OUTWORKING OF HIS KINGDOM. WE HAVE OPPORTUNITIES SERVING IN THIS CAPACITY THAT MANY MISSIONARIES WHO WORK IN A MORE INSTITUTIONAL SETTING NEVER ACHIEVE.

Jonathan and Sarah Bamber

• • • •

INSPIRE MAGAZINE, SUMMER 2021 ISSUE

PURPOSE

GET REALLY GOOD AT WHAT YOU DO. IF YOU'RE AN ACTOR, FIND A GOOD CLASS. **IF YOU'RE A SINGER, TAKE LESSONS.** IF THERE'S AN OPPORTUNITY, GO AHEAD AND STEP INTO IT BECAUSE GETTING ON STAGE, DOING IT, BEING IN THE HOT SEAT, AS MUCH AS YOU CAN, IS GOING TO MAKE YOU BETTER AND BETTER AT YOUR CRAFT. **AND THE BETTER YOU ARE AT YOUR CRAFT, THE MORE PEOPLE ARE GOING TO ENJOY IT.**

Steven Lane

• • • •

INSPIRE PODCAST

The heart is always the reason we do what we do.

Marissa Bell

INSPIRE PODCAST

PURPOSE

My number one goal is to not only help people survive in a digital world, but thrive. . . . How can I help people not be overwhelmed by the digital transformation that's been happening for probably twenty-five years? One of my favorite things regarding technology is to make it simple for people. Technology shouldn't disrupt my life. It should enhance my life. And that's my focus.

Mike Mathews

. . . .

INSPIRE PODCAST

> I LIKE TO SIT DOWN WITH PEOPLE, AND I LIKE TO GIVE THEM HOPE. I LIKE TO HELP THEM TO SEE WHAT IT COULD BE, WHAT IT COULD BE LIKE. AND I ALWAYS TRY TO DISCOURAGE PEOPLE FROM GIVING UP TOO SOON.
>
> Lisa Kai

INSPIRE PODCAST

PURPOSE

MY ASPIRATIONS ARE JUST AS SIMPLE. I WANT TO BE THE BEST KIM IN THE BEST ENVIRONMENT. I DIDN'T COME HERE FOR A POLITICAL ANYTHING. I CAME TO BE A BEACON OF LIFE AND A TRANSFORMER OF SYSTEMS. SO THE NEXT SYSTEM THAT NEEDS TO BE TRANSFORMED, I WILL BE THERE.

Kim Schofield

• • • •

INSPIRE PODCAST

I think the first thing is knowing that God's called you to do what you do. The world doesn't need more copycats. You know, the world needs people who want to present solutions because God has given them the solution.

Josh Duhaylonsod

....

INSPIRE PODCAST

PURPOSE

> If you want to transform your family, seeing the generations after you have a better path, you have to be the transformation. And you have that holistic approach—of body, soul, and spirit. I have to take care of all three of them to be more successful in God's eye.

Gus Mello

....

INSPIRE PODCAST

You need to show up. . . . You need to follow those warmhearted impulses. You need to do the things that you feel called to do—that God's called you to do. Do them with excellence, even if it's as silly as writing stuff on that fence. Significant things can happen even from seemingly insignificant things. The thing that I always say when I talk to folks is, "You don't have to do something grand to do something great." That's my motivation.

Billy Ivey

• • • •

INSPIRE PODCAST

PURPOSE

Prosperity isn't a quick endeavor. Instead, there are things God commands us to do, including stewarding well what we have over the long haul.

Dr. Chris Bowen

....
THE 5-STAR ENTREPRENEUR

FINDING YOUR WHO IS THE MOST LIBERATING FEELING YOU WILL EVER EXPERIENCE. IT GIVES YOU CLARITY, AS WELL AS A SENSE OF MEANING AND PURPOSE IN YOUR LIFE AND IN YOUR CALLING AS A LEADER.

Nicholas John

· · · ·

PILOT

PURPOSE

WE CAN'T ALLOW OURSELVES TO TRY TO LIVE SOMEONE ELSE'S DREAMS. WE CAN BE INSPIRED BY OTHERS, AND WE CAN INSPIRE THEM, BUT EACH PERSON HAS TO OWN HIS OWN DESTINY, PURPOSE, AND GOALS.

Dr. Brenda Chand

• • • •

YOU *CAN COACH*

The ultimate purpose of a resume is to make your phone ring. Hundreds, maybe even thousands, are applying for the job you desire, so you must stand out amongst the competition.

Crystal Marshall

....

INSPIRE MAGAZINE, SPRING 2021 ISSUE

PURPOSE

> I have a heart for people, a mind and instincts for business, and a passion for serving God. God gave me a particular set of experiences, lessons, education, and opportunities, so I could invest them in specific ways.
>
> Krystal Parker

COMMITMENT

CHANGE YOUR WORLD

> A lot of people in the church said church is done in person, not on your phone. But not everyone has the luxury of meeting in person, and don't they deserve connection and help too?

Marissa Bell

....

INSPIRE MAGAZINE, SPRING 2021 ISSUE

COMMITMENT

I've started to understand that true connection and real influence happen when we get real—when we connect through story and begin to look for those small ways we can make a meaningful difference in the lives of others.

Billy Ivey

• • • •

INSPIRE MAGAZINE, SUMMER 2021 ISSUE

> **SO THE REASON THE CHRISTIAN CHAMBER EXISTS IS BECAUSE WE BELIEVE THAT WE HAVE THE ABILITY TO REACH PEOPLE FOR THE KINGDOM THROUGH OUR VOCATION. IF WE DO THAT, WE'RE APT TO BE A PLACE WHERE PEOPLE CAN COME TOGETHER AND GROW IN THEIR FAITH, BUSINESS, AND LEADERSHIP.**
>
> Krystal Parker
>
> *INSPIRE MAGAZINE,* SUMMER 2021 ISSUE

COMMITMENT

It's really hard to do anything solo if you want to really make a difference.

Derek Dienner

• • • •

INSPIRE MAGAZINE, *SPRING 2021 ISSUE*

IT'S SO MUCH BIGGER THAN ANY ONE PERSON. WE ALL HAVE A RESPONSIBILITY, AN OBLIGATION. NONE OF US GOT WHERE WE ARE TODAY ALL ON OUR OWN. WE ALL HAD PEOPLE WHO PLAYED A PART, WHO WERE WAYMAKERS OF SOME KIND, AND WE NEED TO DO AND BE THE SAME FOR OTHERS.

Louis Carr

· · · ·

INSPIRE MAGAZINE, *SUMMER 2021 ISSUE*

WHEN PEOPLE COME TOGETHER AND DEFINE WHICH BEHAVIORS THEY COLLECTIVELY THINK ARE GOOD, BAD, OR SIMPLY TOLERABLE, THEY ESTABLISH A CULTURE. AND ONE OF THE MOST EXCITING PARTS OF LEADING A BUSINESS OR ORGANIZATION IS THE OPPORTUNITY TO SHAPE THE CULTURE FOR THE GROUP OF HUMANS THERE.

Aunie Brooks

• • • •

INSPIRE MAGAZINE, SUMMER 2021 ISSUE

We decide to bless people and help people. That's how pretty much the dream begins.

Gus Mello

····

INSPIRE PODCAST

CHANGE YOUR WORLD

COMMITMENT

> Your vision is your heart. So don't simply tell people about your vision, invite them on a journey with the vision. Inspire them on the journey. Reinvigorate them on the journey. Ask them questions about their journeys.
>
> Dr. Sam Chand

INSPIRE MAGAZINE, SUMMER 2021 ISSUE

I LOVE AND
BELIEVE IN THE
NEXT GENERATION.
I BELIEVE THAT
IT IS OUR JOB
TO POUR INTO
THEM. MY DESIRE
IS JUST TO WORK
TOWARDS BUILDING
A COMMUNITY
OF PEOPLE THAT
BELIEVES IN
POURING INTO THE
NEXT GENERATION,
WHETHER IT'S
THROUGH MINISTRY,
SCHOOLS, OR THEIR
COMMUNITY.

Ty Moody

INSPIRE PODCAST

COMMITMENT

I THINK THAT HAS BEEN A HUGE THING FOR ME, REALIZING I DO NEED GOD MORE THAN I THOUGHT, AND I DO NEED OTHER PEOPLE MORE THAN I THOUGHT. AND IT'S A GOOD THING. I DON'T NEED TO BE INDEPENDENT AND SELF-SUSTAINING LIKE. IT HAS BEEN GOOD TO HUMBLE MYSELF AND TO OPEN MY HEART TO RECEIVING HELP FROM OTHERS.

Tricia Goyer

....

INSPIRE PODCAST

You are only as good as your team. But teams are not self-operating, plug-and-play pieces of equipment you can wind up and then walk away from. They need constant coaching, encouragement, and reminders of the values (that should be stated) about who we are, what we do, why we do it—and most importantly—for Whom we do it.

Mike Kai

••••
IT DOESN'T JUST HAPPEN

COMMITMENT

I think there's a difference between coming to church and coming to a small group and being discipled. There's a difference between going through a ministry school or getting online and getting theology and really having somebody in your life that you are accountable to, that you allow to speak into your blind spots.

Kenneth Claytor

• • • •

INSPIRE PODCAST

I THINK SOMETHING THAT I'VE BEEN LEARNING AND REALLY WORKING ON IS WHO: WHO I AM POURING INTO AND WHO'S POURING INTO ME.

Josh Duhaylonsod

· · · ·

INSPIRE PODCAST

COMMITMENT

No matter what your personal dreams may be, I can promise you that you will never achieve your dreams alone. You will need the advice, the help, the wisdom, and the constructive criticism that others can share with you as you strive to advance your cause.

Dr. Dave Martin

....

MAKE THAT, BREAK THAT

DIVERSE VOICES CAN HELP MAKE YOUR DREAMS COME TRUE. CHURCH EXISTS WHEN MANY COME TOGETHER, CONNECTED BY A SHARED BOND WITH THE DIVINE. IT'S THE POINT WHERE HEAVEN AND EARTH MEET. FIND PEOPLE DIFFERENT FROM YOU THAT MAY EXPRESS NEW ANGLES TO THE DREAM YOU'VE BEEN GIVEN. HUMBLE YOURSELF TO THEIR OPINIONS. INCLUSION BEGINS WITH GENUINE RESPECT FOR OTHER VANTAGE POINTS.

Allison van Tilborgh

....

INSPIRE MAGAZINE, FALL 2021 ISSUE

COMMITMENT

THE PROVERBS 31 WOMAN USES THE SURPLUS OF HER PROFITS TO FEED THE POOR AND PROVIDE FOR THE NEEDY. MEMBERS OF HER HOUSEHOLD, PRESUMABLY INCLUDING SERVANTS (EMPLOYEES), ARE ALL TAKEN CARE OF, WELL CLOTHED AND HAVE NO FEAR ABOUT THE FUTURE.

Hannah J. Stolze

. . . .

WISDOM-BASED BUSINESS: APPLYING BIBLICAL PRINCIPLES AND EVIDENCE-BASED RESEARCH FOR A PURPOSEFUL AND PROFITABLE BUSINESS (ZONDERVAN)

INSPIRATION

CHANGE YOUR WORLD

> **WHAT INSPIRES ME MOST IS PEOPLE AND LEARNING. . . . WHETHER IT'S TALKING TO A MENTOR OR ADVISOR OR FACETIMING WITH FRIENDS, I'M INSPIRED BY WHAT PEOPLE DO CONSISTENTLY. IT TELLS ME A LOT ABOUT WHO THEY WILL BECOME PERMANENTLY, AND BECAUSE I'M ALWAYS OBSERVING AND LEARNING, I'VE NOTICED I WATCH PEOPLE'S HABITS; IT'S HOW I LEARN.**
>
> Micah Cravalho

• • • •

INSPIRE MAGAZINE, SPRING 2021 ISSUE

INSPIRATION

THE HAMILTON SOUNDTRACK (INSPIRES ME). I DRAW STRENGTH FROM THE SONG, "HISTORY HAS ITS EYE ON ME," KNOWING THAT I AM NOT THROWING AWAY MY SHOT. I FIND DAILY JOY IN PSALM 118:23, "THIS IS THE LORD'S DOING; IT IS MARVELOUS IN OUR EYES."

Kim Schofield

• • • •

INSPIRE MAGAZINE, SPRING 2021 ISSUE

The way I get the most inspiration for my personal and professional life is through time spent in God's Word and prayer. In a world that constantly throws major curves along the way through trials, it inspires me to know the truth and wisdom found in God's Word never changes.

John Houston

••••

INSPIRE MAGAZINE, SPRING 2021 ISSUE

INSPIRATION

> WE ARE INSPIRED BY PEOPLE LIVING THEIR BEST LIVES FOR GOD, POINTING TO GOD, HUNGRY FOR HIS KINGDOM HERE AND NOW. WE'RE SURROUNDED BY A GREAT CLOUD OF WITNESSES. IT'S A CONSTANT SOURCE OF ENCOURAGEMENT TO RUN WITH PERSEVERANCE THE RACE MARKED OUT FOR US (HEBREWS 12:1). WE SEE IT LIVED OUT RIGHT BEFORE OUR EYES.

Jonathan and Sarah Bamber

••••

INSPIRE MAGAZINE, *SUMMER 2021 ISSUE*

There's simply nothing better (for inspiration) than a great story, well told. My favorite storytellers are usually songwriters; that someone can capture my attention and make me listen, hum, tap my foot and sing a story in less than three minutes has always been fascinating to me. My go-to these days (and for the past several years) are The Avett Brothers. I love everything they put out, but if you want a great example of beautiful storytelling, go listen to the album *I and Love and You.*

Billy Ivey

INSPIRATION

A quote that constantly inspires me to dig deeper and strive harder for bigger and better things in business and my personal development is from Charlie "Tremendous" Jones: "You'll be the same person in five years as you are today except for the people you meet and the books you read."

Dr. Chris Bowen

THE BEST CALLS TO ACTION ARE BY TURN INSPIRATIONAL, ASPIRATIONAL, AND INSTRUCTIONAL. FIRST, THEY INSPIRE YOU WITH A VISION OF SOMETHING OR SOMEONE THAT MAKES AN IMPRESSION. THEN THEY CAUSE YOU TO ASPIRE TO SOMETHING SIMILAR; MAYBE YOU COULD BE LIKE THEM! AND FINALLY, THEY GIVE SOME INSTRUCTION ON HOW YOU CAN ACHIEVE THAT GOAL.

Andy Butcher

••••

INSPIRE MAGAZINE, SUMMER 2021 ISSUE

GREAT WORSHIP MUSIC (INSPIRES ME). THERE ARE SO MANY AMAZING SONGS DERIVED FROM THE BIBLE; LISTENING, WORSHIPING, AND SINGING ALONG HELPS ME. **IT CENTERS ME, IT LIFTS ME, AND IT QUIETS ME, SO I CAN HEAR FROM GOD.** ELEVATION WORSHIP (PRODUCED BY ELEVATION CHURCH IN CHARLOTTE, NORTH CAROLINA) IS ON REPLAY!

Krystal Parker

• • • •

INSPIRE MAGAZINE, SUMMER 2021 ISSUE

Mockingbird—mbird.com, "connecting the Christian faith with the realities of everyday life"—inspires me. They can talk theology. They can also talk Beavis and Butt-Head. Wherever they can find truth or the gospel or the lack thereof, they're talking about it, and I find life and freedom there.

Steven Lane

....

INSPIRE MAGAZINE, SUMMER 2021 ISSUE

INSPIRATION

> People like Elon Musk and Michael Jordan (inspire me). I like to grasp onto the way they think, talk, and interpret the world they're in and how they assess and take on challenges. For me, it doesn't always have to be overtly "spiritual."
>
> Christian Taylor

....

INSPIRE MAGAZINE, SUMMER 2021 ISSUE

(I'M INSPIRED BY) LOUIS ARMSTRONG'S MASTERPIECE, "WHAT A WONDERFUL WORLD," WITH ITS MESSAGE: "I SEE TREES OF GREEN, RED ROSES TOO, I SEE THEM BLOOM, FOR ME AND FOR YOU, AND I THINK TO MYSELF, WHAT A WONDERFUL WORLD." FOR ME, IT ECHOES IDEAS FROM PSALM 103. THE FIRST LINE REMINDS ME OF THE BEAUTY ALIVE EVEN NOW IN A FALLEN WORLD.

Michael Ray Smith

••••

INSPIRE MAGAZINE, SUMMER 2021 ISSUE

INSPIRATION

I READ THE BOOK OF PROVERBS THROUGH EVERY MONTH, ONE CHAPTER PER DAY. IT GIVES ME INSPIRATION FOR NEW THINGS. I GET NEW INSIGHT AND WISDOM EVERY MONTH, AND I CHALLENGE ALL OF MY BUSINESS CLIENTS AND PROTÉGÉS TO TAKE THE CHALLENGE AND WATCH THE CREATIVE THOUGHTS AND IDEAS FOR THE BUSINESS THAT COME FROM IT.

Dr. Dave Martin

• • • •

MAKE THAT, BREAK THAT

I realized very quickly that at my new company, integrating faith and work was just as much a part of the culture as was greeting people with smiles and hugs. Over the course of that first year, not only did I find the company's practices to be perfectly legal, but as a woman of faith myself, I found the culture to be very liberating.

Aunie Brooks

· · · ·

INSPIRE MAGAZINE, SUMMER 2021 ISSUE

INSPIRATION

I'm really inspired about INSPIRE.

Dr. Sam Chand

••••
INSPIRE PODCAST

GIFTS

CHANGE YOUR WORLD

WE ARE EACH GIVEN ONE LIFE. WE EACH HAVE A SPECIAL GIFT TO SHARE WITH OTHERS, WHETHER IT'S IN THE ARTS, FINANCES, LEADERSHIP, ENTREPRENEURSHIP, OR GOVERNMENT. HOW WILL WE LIVE OUT THE STORY GOD HAS INTENDED FOR US TO LIVE?

Lisa Kai

• • • •

INSPIRE MAGAZINE, *SPRING 2021 ISSUE*

> Your voice is the most powerful gift that you have. What's aligned in your heart comes out through your mind and your mouth.
>
> Kim Schofield

INSPIRE MAGAZINE, SPRING 2021 ISSUE

AS A CHRIST-FOLLOWER, AS A CEO, AS A LEADER, IT IS MY RESPONSIBILITY TO COME PREPARED TO GIVE EVERYONE THE HOPE THAT'S WITHIN ME.

John Houston

· · · ·

INSPIRE MAGAZINE, SPRING 2021 ISSUE

GIFTS

I FIND SO MUCH JOY IN ACTING FOR HIM. THAT'S AN INDICATOR FOR ME OF WHO GOD IS—THAT WHEN WE ARE IN OUR GIFTING, WE COME ALIVE.

Steven Lane

••••

INSPIRE MAGAZINE, SUMMER 2021 ISSUE

> My heart is ministry. Everything else I do to keep myself afloat, whether it's art on somebody's head or art on a wall, a couch, a shoe, or whatever. Creativity is a gift the Lord has given me, and I enjoy it, but I come alive when I can really minister to people.

Ada Madison

····

INSPIRE MAGAZINE, SUMMER 2021 ISSUE

GIFTS

I love to sing, or I love to act, or whatever it is. If you're drawn to that, and you can do that well, and you feel alive, there's something special about that. I feel that glorifies God. It's a real demonstration of who He is.

Steven Lane

....

INSPIRE PODCAST

WE REALLY WANTED TO USE OUR DIGITAL TALENTS, EXPERTISE, AND EXPERIENCE TO HELP BRING NEW GENERATIONS CLOSER TO GOD AND CLOSER TO THE FAITH. IT'S SO IMPORTANT, ESPECIALLY IN THIS DAY AND AGE.

Marissa Bell

INSPIRE PODCAST

I THINK THE BIGGEST OBSTACLE WAS OVERCOMING MY STRENGTHS. ... I KNEW I WAS A STRONG PERSON IN SOME WAYS— STRONG IN MY OPINION, STRONG IN MY IDEAS. I'VE LEARNED HOW TO UTILIZE THAT AS A GIFT VERSUS THINKING IT'S SOMETHING THAT'S NOT GOOD.

Lisa Kai

· · · ·

INSPIRE PODCAST

What I would say to people who are called into public service or an elected capacity is to know this: Your gift makes room for you. You cannot hide the light that you shine. It's bigger than your personal desire and your need. It is a calling that is mandating you to step into a space. When we truly understand that about servanthood, nothing else matters.

Kim Schofield

....

INSPIRE PODCAST

GIFTS

How many categories do you think God has for His people? The answer is so simple yet so hard for us to understand. His portfolio of categories for His children is endless. There is no end to His diversity in the plans and purposes He has for us. By unique, authentic, divine design we all are created different. We are endowed with gifts that have been given to us and to nobody else. Therefore, I need to play a role in the earth that only I can play. You are a gift sent by God to the world.

Martijn van Tilborgh

SOME PEOPLE ARE NATURALLY GIFTED IN ESTABLISHING CLEAR BENCHMARKS OF PROGRESS, BUT MOST PEOPLE NEED SOME HELP TO CLARIFY THE DESTINATION AND THE PATH TO GET THERE.

Dr. Brenda Chand

• • • •

YOU *CAN COACH*

GIFTS

So, don't be like most people. Be exceptional! Don't be like most people. Be great!

Dr. Dave Martin

• • • •

MAKE THAT, BREAK THAT

WHETHER IT BE YOUR ROLE AS A REAL ESTATE AGENT, A YOUTHMIN PASTOR, OR A VOLUNTEER AT A SOUP KITCHEN, IT IS IMPERATIVE THAT YOU RECOGNIZE THE GIFT YOU'VE BEEN GIVEN, IN THE FORM OF YOUR VISIONS.

Allison van Tilborgh

· · · ·

INSPIRE MAGAZINE, FALL 2021 ISSUE

GIFTS

THE HOLY SPIRIT WILL GIVE ME AN IMAGE. I CLEARLY SEE IT, AND I TURN INTO RAIN MAN. I CAN'T STOP. I PUT EVERYTHING ASIDE 'TILL I PAINT IT.

Ada Madison

....

INSPIRE MAGAZINE, *SUMMER 2021 ISSUE*

www.ingramcontent.com/pod-product-compliance
Lightning Source LLC
Chambersburg PA
CBHW070048100426
42734CB00040B/2787